NEW TESTAMENT
HIDDEN PICTURES

TO FIND AND COLOR

ILLUSTRATED BY KIT WRAY

STANDARD
PUBLISHING
Cincinnati, Ohio

Jesus Is Born

While Joseph and Mary were in Bethlehem, the time came for her to have the baby. There were no rooms left in the inn. So Mary wrapped the baby with cloths and laid him in a box where animals are fed.

Luke 2:6, 7

Find a star, robin's head, a turkey, man-in-the-moon, and a slice of bread.

Find a sea gull, bowl, puppy, frog, and frying pan.

Find a cat, chicken, shield, cardinal, and a shark.

Shepherds Hear About Jesus

That night, some shepherds were in the fields nearby watching their sheep. An angel of the Lord stood before them. The angel said to them, "Don't be afraid, because I am bringing you some good news. Today your Savior was born in David's town."

Luke 2:8-11

Find a spear, whale, heart, head of a pig, and a humming bird.

Jesus Teaches the Teachers

When Jesus was twelve years old, he went with his parents to Jerusalem for the Passover feast. There he sat in the temple talking with the religious teachers. All who heard him were amazed at his understanding and wise answers. Luke 2:41-47

Find a cane, a banana, a mouse, a plate, and a horn.

John Teaches People About Jesus

John was Jesus' cousin. He had prepared all his life to be a teacher and when he was old enough, he began telling others that someone wonderful was coming. "Prepare the way for the Lord," John said. "Make straight paths for him." He was talking about Jesus. When people were sorry for their sins, and decided to stop sinning, John baptized them. For this reason, he was called, "John the Baptist."

Luke 1:11-17; Matthew 3:1-6

Find the head of a donkey, a squirrel, a hamster, a glove, and a lizard.

Find a pie, gopher, bird, broom, and a lamb's head.

8

Jesus Chooses His Students

Jesus was walking by Lake Galilee. He saw two brothers, Simon and Andrew, fishing with a net, and two other brothers, James and John, fishing with their father from a boat. Jesus said, "Come, follow me. I will make you fishermen for men."

Matthew 4:18-22

Find a horse head, an ax, oar, ram's head, and lion's head.

Jesus Is a Friend of Children

When Jesus was teaching big crowds of people, some parents brought their children to Jesus so that he could bless them. The students thought that Jesus was too busy for this, so they told the parents to stop. But Jesus said, "Let the little children come to me. The kingdom of God belongs to people who are like these little children."

Mark 10:13-16

Find a fish, dove, shovel, candle, and a jug.

Jesus Is Kind to Zacchaeus

Zacchaeus was a wealthy, important man. He wanted to see Jesus, but he was too short to see above the crowd. So, he climbed a sycamore tree. When Jesus came by, he saw Zacchaeus. "Come down!" Jesus said, "I must stay at your house today."
Luke 19:1-9

Find a lizard, camel's head, hawk's head, chipmunk, and a bull's head.

Find a fork, bear's head, alligator's head, arrow, and a pear.

Jesus Heals a Paralyzed Man

Because Jesus had healed so many people, more and more sick people came to him. Some men brought their friend, who was paralyzed, but the crowd around Jesus was so thick that they could not get close. These men carried their friend up to the roof of the house where Jesus was and knocked a hole in the roof! Then they lowered their friend down into the room, and Jesus healed him.

Mark 2:1-12

Find a carrot, a pot, a sword, a bird's head, and a snake.

Find a nail, dolphin, wolf head, kangaroo, and a cooking pot.

Jesus Stops a Storm

Jesus had been teaching all day and was very tired. He got into a boat with his students and fell asleep. While he was sleeping, a terrible storm started and created waves so big that they broke over the sides of the boat. The students were terrified. "Wake up!" they said to Jesus, "Don't you care if we drown?" But Jesus said to the waves, "Quiet! Be still!" Then the wind died down and the lake was completely calm.

Mark 4:35-39

Find a rooster, parrot, spoon, hammer, and two bowls.

Jesus Brings His Friend Back to Life

Jesus was sad that Lazarus had died. He came to the tomb, looked up and said, "Father, I want these people to believe that you sent me." Then he said, "Lazarus, come out!" And Lazarus, who had been dead, came out of the tomb.

John 11:38-43

Find a crow, dolphin, shovel, sea horse, and a snail.

Mary Gives Jesus an Expensive Gift

Mary and Martha were sisters of Lazarus and they were all close friends of Jesus. After Jesus raised Lazarus from the dead, Mary and Martha gave a dinner in honor of Jesus. Martha served the meal. Mary poured an expensive bottle of perfume on Jesus' feet and wiped his feet with her hair. The sweet scent filled the whole house.   John 12:1-3

Find a ring, a feather, an egg, the head of a cow, and a caterpillar.

Jesus Teaches About Giving

A woman put two small coins into the temple money box. Jesus said, "This poor widow gave more than all those rich people. The rich have plenty; they gave only what they did not need. This woman is very poor and she needed that money to live, but she gave all she had."

Luke 21:1-4

Find a puppy's head, a frog's head, a seal, a bear, a sickle, and a traveling bag.

Jesus Returns to Heaven

After Jesus was killed on a cross, and God brought him back to life, he stayed with his friends and followers for forty days. He taught them more about what would happen and said that the Holy Spirit would come to help them. He told his followers to go all over the world teaching others about God, his Son, and the Holy Spirit. Then, while his followers were watching, Jesus was taken up into Heaven.

Acts 1:6-11

Find a rabbit head, a goose head, a kangaroo, deer head, and a duck.

Saul Believes Who Jesus Is

Saul was a Jew who was serious about serving God, but he did not believe that Jesus was the Messiah. He arrested those who did believe and had them killed. He was on his way to arrest more followers of Jesus when a bright light from Heaven blinded him. Saul heard a voice saying, "Why are you doing things against me? I am Jesus, the One you are trying to hurt." Saul was blind for several days but then he realized that Jesus was the Messiah, and he began to tell others what was true.

Acts 9:1-22

Find a hatchet, a toucan head, the letter "X," a lamb, and a mouse head.

Saul Becomes a Great Teacher

Saul, who soon became known as Paul, traveled all over the world telling people that Jesus is the Son of God. God protected Paul from all kinds of trouble so that he could continue teaching. Once, the ship that Paul was on sank, but all the people aboard were able to swim to an island. There, it was raining and cold so they built a fire. Paul reached for some sticks to add to the fire and a poisonous snake latched onto his hand. Everyone expected Paul to die but he simply shook the snake off into the fire.

Acts 27:39-28:6

Find a lizard, a frog, a pen, an eagle head, and a goose head.

21

God's Word Goes Around the World

Paul and the men with him went throughout Asia and Syria teaching about Jesus. In a dream, a man said to Paul, "Come over to Macedonia (now called Greece). Help us!" Paul immediately went to Philippi where he talked with a woman named Lydia. Lydia worshipped the true God and she and all the people in her house were baptized.

Acts 16:6-15

Find a comb, a sandal, a bottle, a bee, a mouse, and a rhinoceros head.

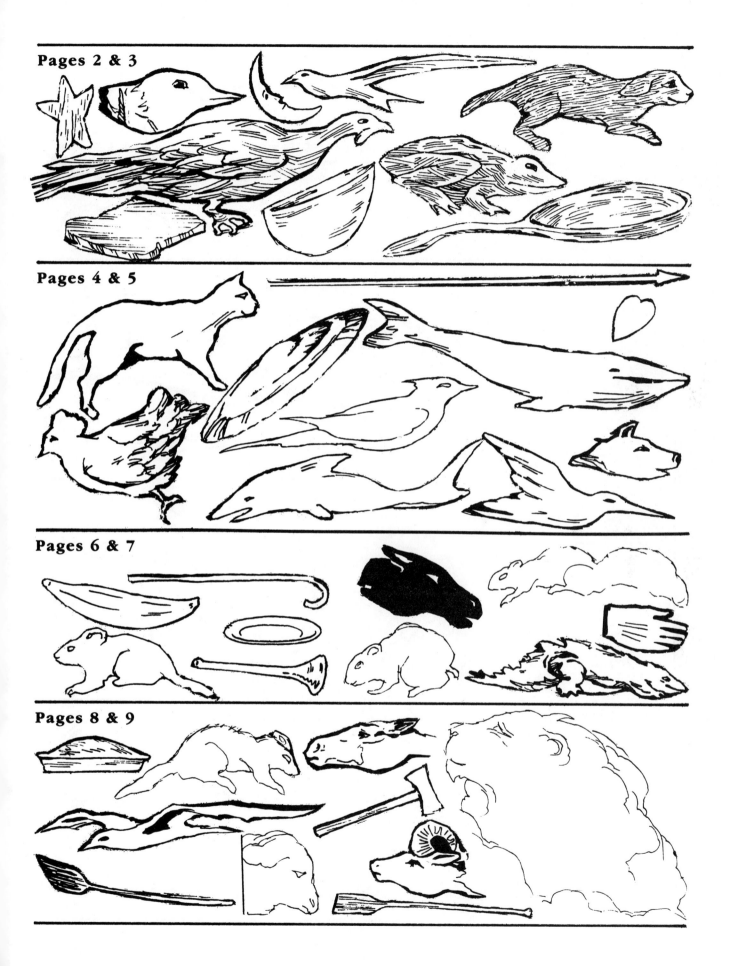

Pages 2 & 3

Pages 4 & 5

Pages 6 & 7

Pages 8 & 9

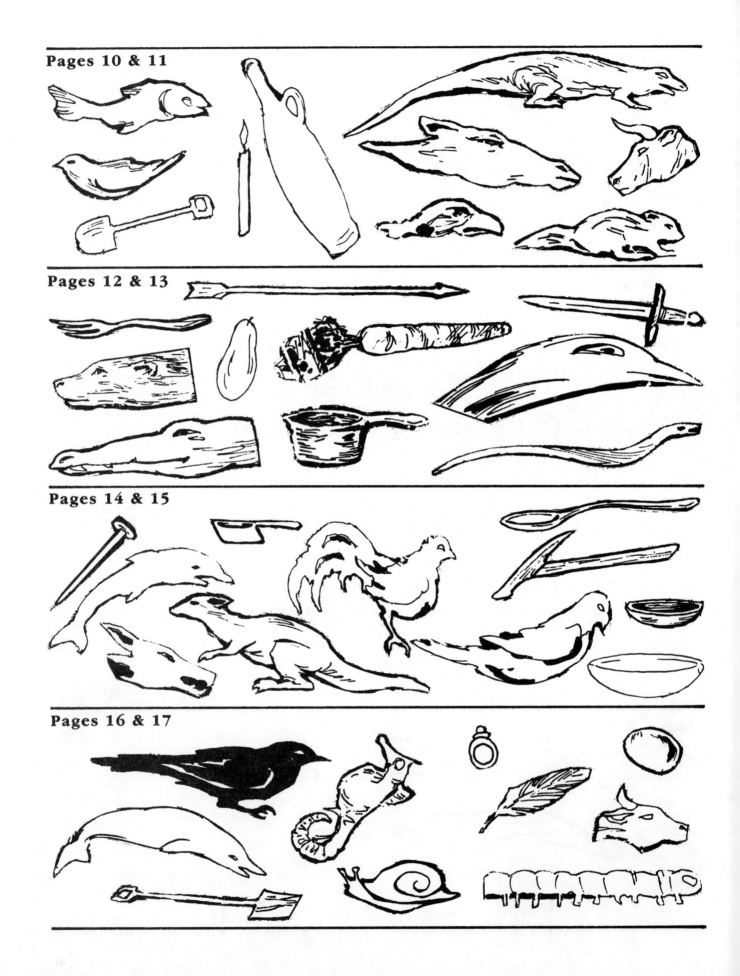

Pages 10 & 11

Pages 12 & 13

Pages 14 & 15

Pages 16 & 17